Where Is Niagara Falls?

by Megan Stine

illustrated by Tim Foley

Grosset & Dunlap
An Imprint of Penguin Random House

For Betsy, Gail, Jean, and Sue—
Yours till Niagara Falls—MS

GROSSET & DUNLAP
Penguin Young Readers Group
An Imprint of Penguin Random House LLC

Text copyright © 2015 by Megan Stine. Illustrations copyright © 2015 by
Penguin Random House LLC. All rights reserved. Published by Grosset & Dunlap, an
imprint of Penguin Random House LLC, 345 Hudson Street, New York, New York 10014.
GROSSET & DUNLAP is a trademark of Penguin Random House LLC.
Printed in the USA.

Library of Congress Cataloging-in-Publication Data is available.

ISBN 978-0-448-48425-9   10 9 8 7 6 5 4 3 2 1

Contents

Where Is Niagara Falls?

It was a beautiful, hot summer afternoon in 1960. Seven-year-old Roger Woodward was excited. He and his older sister Deanne were about to go on a boat ride. It was Roger's first time ever in a boat. They were going out onto the Niagara River in a motorboat that was just big enough to hold three people.

"Remember to wear your life jacket," Roger's father called out to him. His father knew they needed to be careful. They were going on a river that led to the biggest, most awesome waterfall in America.

The man who owned the boat was a family friend named Jim Honeycutt. Jim was a strong swimmer and lifeguard. He knew all about how to stay safe on the river. He made sure Roger kept his life jacket on.

As they passed under a bridge, Roger asked if he could steer the boat. It was a bad idea to let Roger steer right then. The boat was nearing a dangerous part of the river. Most boaters knew to turn around there. The river was full of rocks and rapids that led to the edge of Niagara Falls.

But for some reason, Jim said yes.

Suddenly, the boat hit something hard under

the water. The engine screamed. A piece of the motor was broken. They couldn't drive the boat away from the rocks. The rapids were pulling them toward the edge!

Jim grabbed some oars and began to row as hard as he could. He shouted to Deanne to put on the only other life jacket in the boat. Powerful waves tossed them up and down. When a huge one hit the boat, all three were thrown into the swirling, raging rapids.

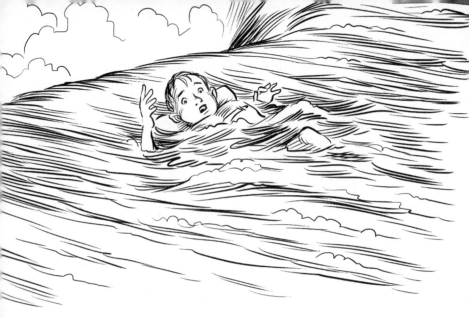

Roger tried to hold on to Jim, but the water ripped him away.

People on the shore saw what was happening. They ran up and down, but no one could figure out a way to help.

Roger felt himself being bounced against rocks. Then he was dragged over the edge of the gigantic falls, like a fly being flushed down a toilet.

No one had ever survived going over Niagara Falls without something—a boat or a barrel—to protect them.

But somehow, a miracle happened! Roger found himself floating in the water below the falls. A tourist boat happened to be nearby. Someone spotted Roger's red life jacket and fished him out of the water. He was saved!

Roger became famous that day. He was the first person ever to survive going over Niagara Falls

Roger and Deanne as adults

without protection. When he grew up, he became a sailor. He loved the water and even joined the navy. His sister survived that day, too. She was pulled out of the river before ever reaching the falls.

But Jim Honeycutt died in the terrible accident. Sadly, he was not the first—or last—to lose his life to the biggest, most awesome, and most dangerous waterfall in America.

CHAPTER 1
A Terrible Beauty

The first people to see Niagara Falls were Native Americans.

We don't know for sure what happened, but we can imagine.

At some point, Native Americans probably paddled a canoe along the peaceful river that divided two pieces of land—what is now the

United States and Canada. Suddenly, the water began to run a little faster. They probably heard a noise. What was it? Rushing water! Before they knew it, they were being pulled toward the edge!

They might have paddled toward the riverbank. Some might have reached safety. Others might have gotten caught up in the rushing rapids, gone over the falls, and died.

Or perhaps the first Native Americans came upon the falls on foot. Imagine their surprise at seeing a huge wall of crashing water!

We know that was the reaction of the first white man who saw Niagara Falls.

In 1678, a French priest named Father Louis Hennepin set out with a group of men from Europe. They traveled through Canada, across the river from what is now New York State. The men wanted to build a fort near the river. As they pushed their way through the trees, they saw a huge mist. Then they saw the gigantic falls—Niagara Falls!

The wall of water was more than 160 feet high—as high as a fifteen-story building. And it was twenty times as wide as it was high! It was actually three waterfalls stretching across the river, not just one. Together they were more than half a mile wide.

Father Hennepin was so terrified when he saw the falls, he began shaking. He dropped to his knees and started praying. When he glanced at the falls again, he quickly turned his head away.

He was too frightened even to keep looking! Later
he said he was "seized with horror."

Father Louis Hennepin

When he got home, Father Hennepin wrote about Niagara Falls. He called it the "most beautiful and at the same time most frightful cascade in the world." He said the sound of it was "more terrible than thunder!"

Seventy years later, a Swedish man named Pehr Kalm saw Niagara Falls. In 1751, his travel diary was printed in English. He said, "You cannot see it without being quite terrified."

Pehr Kalm

The bodies of dead bears and deer were found at the bottom of the falls. Even birds flying over Niagara Falls got so wet from the spray, they were sucked into the falls and killed!

Soon, Niagara Falls became a place that everyone in the world wanted to see. But what would they find when they got there?

Nature at Work

Two million years ago, the earth was covered with ice. As the huge sheets of ice melted and moved over time, they dug into the earth and carved out rivers and lakes.

The Great Lakes and Niagara Falls were both formed this way, about ten thousand years ago. The Great Lakes are huge—they hold one-fifth of all the freshwater on earth. The water in the lakes is always running toward the sea. The water from the four biggest lakes—Superior, Michigan, Huron, and Erie—flows into the fifth lake, Lake Ontario. But first, all that water has to move down the Niagara River and over the edge of a cliff. The flow of the water over that cliff created Niagara Falls.

Why are there three falls instead of just one?

Millions of gallons of water rush down the Niagara River. But right at the lip of the cliff, there's

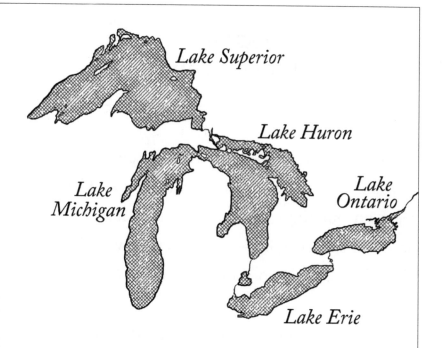

Lake Superior

Lake Huron

Lake Michigan

Lake Ontario

Lake Erie

an island in the way. That island is called Goat Island. It forces the water to go around it on either side.

On the west side of Goat Island, the water creates the Canadian Falls, also called the Horseshoe Falls. It's the biggest waterfall at Niagara. On the east side, another small island divides the falls into two parts—the American Falls and a smaller waterfall called Bridal Veil Falls.

CHAPTER 2
A Town Is Born

In the early days, when visitors came to see Niagara Falls, it was a wild, natural spot. There were no buildings nearby. There was no bridge across the deep gorge—the valley between the cliffs. There were no stairs leading down to the river.

Some men and women were adventurous, though. They wanted to see the falls from every side—even if it was dangerous! In the late 1700s, a few men hiked and climbed down the steep cliffs beside Niagara Falls. They wanted to see the waterfall from below. They climbed down a series of ladders that Native Americans had left behind. The ladders were just a series of tree trunks with tomahawk notches cut into them!

When the men reached the bottom, they
decided to walk behind the waterfall. Inching
along, they made their way to the gap between
the cliff wall and the sheet of water. But when
they got there, they could hardly breathe! The
spray was like being in a steam bath. And the
wind from a cave behind the falls sucked all the
air away.

A few years later, in 1795, the wife of a Canadian governor wanted to climb down to the gorge. So a better ladder was built for her. This one was just a bunch of logs tied together with grapevines! It dangled out from the edge of the cliff, over the gorge. Some brave men were terrified at the thought of it. But the governor's wife climbed down it in full, floor-length skirts!

Pretty soon, people were coming from all over to see Niagara Falls. Roads were built. Hotels were built.

One man, Augustus Porter, bought a lot of land on the American side of the falls. He also bought Goat Island. He wanted to make sure it stayed wild and beautiful.

Augustus Porter

Goat Island had been named after the goats that once lived there. The mist from the falls kept the plants fresh and green. Beautiful wildflowers and ferns grew everywhere. When other men wanted to build a tavern on Goat Island, Porter said no. He kept it natural so that people could enjoy it for many years to come.

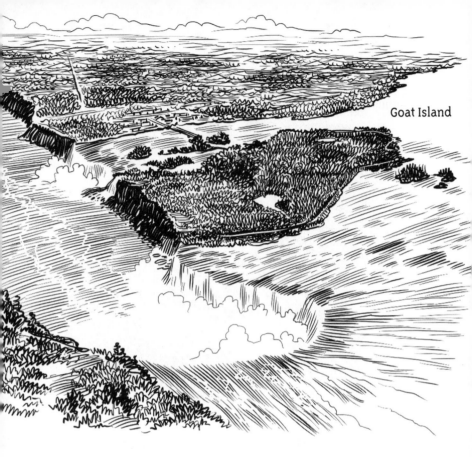

Goat Island

But the rest of the land near Niagara Falls was another story. Porter built a blacksmith shop, a tannery, and a tavern. He built a bridge to Goat Island and charged people to walk across it. He also built a sawmill that used the force of the falling water as power to run the saws.

When Porter's daughter traveled to Europe on vacation, a man asked her if she had seen Niagara Falls.

"I own them," she replied.

The Hermit of Niagara

In 1829, a young man named Francis Abbott arrived at Niagara Falls on foot. He was carrying a flute, a book, and some blankets. After taking one look at the falls, he knew he couldn't leave. For many years Augustus Porter let him live in an old log cabin on Goat Island.

Abbott let his hair grow long and walked around in bare feet, wrapped in a blanket. He didn't shave. Sometimes he wouldn't speak to people—he'd only write on a chalkboard. He wrote in his journals all the time and made drawings. Sometimes he shocked people by walking on a narrow wooden plank that led over the edge of the falls. He would hang by his hands over the falls for up to fifteen minutes! Pretty soon, people began calling him the Hermit of Niagara.

One day, after he'd been there two years, Abbott folded his clothes on the banks of the river below the falls. Then he climbed into the water. A ferry boatman saw him go under, but he never came back up. His body was found in the river eleven days later.

When local people went back to his cabin, they found his dog guarding the door. Inside were his musical instruments and blank pieces of paper. None of his drawings or writings was left behind. All that was left of the hermit were the stories people told about his strange life there. After he died, his favorite swimming spot near Goat Island was named Hermit's Cascade.

CHAPTER 3
A Boy, a Kite, and a Bridge

Before long, other men like Porter came to Niagara Falls and started building hotels, shops, houses, and restaurants. A man named William Forsyth built a fancy hotel on the Canadian side, called the Pavilion Hotel. He also built a covered

Pavilion Hotel

walkway that led down the steep cliff to the foot
of the falls. Now tourists could get a good view at
the bottom without risking their lives on the way
down! At the bottom, they could walk behind the
falls and stand behind the huge curtain of water.
They could also walk into the Cave of the Winds
behind the waterfall.

Pretty soon, Niagara Falls became a huge tourist attraction. By 1845, more than fifty thousand people were coming to see it every year.

A ferryboat was built to take people from the US side to Canada. It was named the *Maid of the Mist*, because it sailed through all the mist and spray coming from the waterfall.

But there was still one thing missing—something the businessmen knew they needed. They needed a bridge so that tourists could cross the gorge.

There was only one problem. Even at the narrowest spot, the gorge was eight hundred feet wide. To build a bridge, a sturdy cable had to stretch across the two cliffs. How could that be done?

The water below the cliffs was too choppy. The Whirlpool Rapids were right where they wanted to build the bridge. If a boat tried to take the cable across the river, the rapids would swallow up the boat.

One man, an engineer named Charles Ellet Jr., had some ideas. At first he thought about shooting a rocket from one side of the gorge to the other. If the rocket had a rope attached, that would do the trick. Or maybe he could shoot a cannonball out of a cannon, with a rope attached!

Then someone came up with a better idea. Why not hold a kite-flying contest? Maybe someone could fly a kite from one side of the river and make it land on the other side. The thin kite string would be stretched across the gorge. Then a thicker string could be tied to the end of the kite string in Canada. Someone in America would pull it across the gorge. After that, thicker and thicker ropes would be tied and pulled across. Eventually, Ellet would be able to pull a thick metal cable across the gorge. The thick cable was the first step in building a suspension bridge.

Charles Ellet Jr.

What Is a Suspension Bridge?

Many famous bridges, including the Golden Gate Bridge and the Brooklyn Bridge, are suspension bridges. A suspension bridge is built so that the weight of the roadway or "deck" of the bridge is held up by cables. The cables are supported by two tall towers—one on each side of a waterway. The towers must be very strong, built out of stone, bricks, or concrete.

tower

cable

The two main cables hang down in an arch from the top of the towers. All the weight of the bridge is suspended—or hangs down—from them. Smaller cables dangle from the main cables and hold up the deck of the bridge.

Golden Gate Bridge

deck

The kite-flying contest was announced. Ellet offered a prize of ten dollars. That was a lot of money in 1848. A sixteen-year-old boy named Homan Walsh was one of the contestants.

Homan lived in the United States, but he knew the winds were best on the Canadian side of the river. On a cold day in January, Homan took a ferryboat over to Canada. Then he walked two miles downriver to where the bridge was going to be built. He put his kite up in the air and let it drift across the river.

All day long, Homan let out balls of string, so his kite would reach the far shore. Then he waited. At midnight, the wind would die down. His kite

would fall on the American side. He would win!

But when the kite fell to the ground, the string broke!

Now Homan was stranded in Canada at midnight, alone. And he couldn't get back home because there was too much ice on the river! The ferryboats weren't running.

For the next eight days, Homan had to stay in Canada. Luckily, some nice people took him in. When the ferryboats were finally running again, he went back to the US side and found his kite. He fixed the broken string. Then he went back to Canada and tried again.

This time, it worked. His kite reached the far
shore, and Homan Walsh won the contest!

Charles Ellet Jr. built a temporary bridge across the gorge, but it was only the first of many. John Roebling, a famous bridge builder, finished the bridge over Niagara Falls. Later, he went on to build the Brooklyn Bridge.

John Roebling

As the years went by, some Niagara bridges collapsed, and some had to be rebuilt several times. Sometimes bridges fell because the ice on the river jammed into the bridge supports and knocked them down. Sometimes strong winds and storms did damage.

A sign on John Roebling's bridge warned that people would be fined if they galloped their horses across the bridge. There was also a fine for marching in step, or marching to music!

But the Ellet bridge was the beginning. And from the bridge, tourists had a perfect view of the crazy, dangerous things some people would soon do at Niagara Falls.

The Day Niagara Falls Went Dry

Just a few months after Homan Walsh flew his kite across the gorge, something strange and terrifying happened. All of a sudden, just after midnight on March 29, 1848, Niagara Falls went dry! Millions of gallons of water had been rushing across the falls for thousands of years. That night, it just stopped.

People woke up in their beds—because of the silence! They were so used to the sound of rushing water, the quiet woke them up.

Everyone went outside to see what had happened. To their amazement, there was no water in the river. No water rushing over the falls. They could walk right across the dry riverbed!

At first, no one could explain what had happened. People went to church and prayed. They thought the end of the world had come! But before long—about a day later—the water came rushing back.

What had happened?

An unusually strong wind had blown huge chunks of ice across Lake Erie. The ice formed a dam. It blocked the water from flowing out of Lake Erie and into the Niagara River. When the ice jam cleared, the water came rushing back.

Niagara Falls was back in business. The world wasn't going to end after all.

CHAPTER 4
Daredevils

As soon as crowds of people started coming to see the falls, the daredevils showed up, too. Daredevils are people willing to do something risky to become famous. And what better place to take a risk than at the most powerful waterfall in America?

Sam Patch was the first daredevil to show off at Niagara Falls. Sam was known as the Jersey Jumper. He jumped from high places in New Jersey into rivers and lakes.

In 1829, a poster appeared in Niagara. It said that Sam Patch would "leap at the falls" on Saturday, October 17, at exactly three o'clock. When the day came, he climbed onto a platform by the cliffs of Goat Island. The platform stuck out about one hundred feet above the falls.

With huge crowds watching from both shores, Patch took off his shoes and kissed a flag. Then he jumped!

"He's dead!" people screamed.

But a minute later, his head came up, bobbing in the water. Somehow, he had survived the crazy jump into Niagara Falls.

Sam Patch wasn't as lucky on his next jump. When he tried to leap from another waterfall about seventy-five miles away, he hit the water and was killed.

The next daredevil at Niagara was a French tightrope walker named Blondin. Blondin came to see Niagara Falls one summer. He took one look at the falls and set his heart on walking across the dangerously high space—on a rope!

The very next year, in 1859, he stretched a rope more than a thousand feet long across the gorge and announced what he planned to do.

Everyone thought Blondin was crazy for taking such a chance. The *New York Times* called Blondin a fool. They thought he should be arrested for even trying this stunt!

Twenty-five thousand people came to see what would happen. Amazingly, Blondin didn't just walk across the rope, though. He danced across it. He leaped. He did somersaults. He balanced on a chair. He even walked across blindfolded!

He also wore fantastic costumes for each performance. One day he appeared as a gorilla. Once, he carried his manager across the rope on his back, piggyback style! He even carried a small stove on his back to the middle of the rope. There, Blondin stopped and cooked an egg on the stove. Then he lowered the dish to a tour boat waiting below, so someone could eat it!

Blondin made money from his stunts. He passed a hat around after each act to collect money. But the hotels nearby made even more money. They charged tourists to sit in special chairs to watch Blondin's terrifying act.

A year after Blondin's first stunt, another daredevil showed up. His real name was William Leonard Hunt, but he used the stage name "Farini."

William Leonard Hunt

Farini wanted to do everything Blondin did, and more. He copied a lot of Blondin's daring acts, adding his own twist. Instead of cooking an egg on the tightrope, Farini brought a washtub with him. Teetering on the tightrope, high above the Niagara River, he lowered the washtub down to have it filled with water. Then he hauled it back up—and washed ladies' handkerchiefs in it!

All summer long, Farini and Blondin competed with each other. Farini tried to top Blondin by hanging upside down by his legs. He even let the tightrope go slack. Then he walked across it while it was swaying in the breeze.

Blondin was more popular with the crowds. Farini, however, was a smarter businessman. He got everyone to pay him for his stunts—even the railroad and steamship owners! They paid him because he was bringing more tourists to Niagara Falls. One day in 1860, he made fifteen thousand dollars for just one hour's work!

The two daredevils were so famous that an English prince came to see them. They both offered to carry the prince across the gorge on the tightrope. The prince said no thanks.

After that, all kinds of people tried to become famous by facing the falls. But who would guess that the next daredevil—the most famous one of all—would be a little old woman with gray hair?

CHAPTER 5
Over Niagara Falls in a Barrel

It was a crazy idea—going over Niagara Falls in a barrel!

But when Annie Edson Taylor heard someone had tried and failed, she decided to try it herself.

Actually, no one had tried it. A man named Carlisle Graham *claimed* he went over the falls in a barrel—but it wasn't true.

Annie Edson
Taylor

Carlisle Graham had ridden inside a very large handmade barrel through the Whirlpool Rapids on the river below the falls.

Graham rode through the rapids four times. On his fifth ride, he told everyone he would start at the top and go over the falls—but he didn't.

Annie Edson Taylor read about Graham's daring stunts and got an idea. She decided that she would do what no man had done before. If she could survive going over Niagara Falls in a barrel, she would be famous.

Carlisle Graham

People would pay to meet her and hear her talk about her amazing, dangerous trick.

Annie's plan was even crazier, because she was a chubby, sixty-three-year-old woman. She had been a schoolteacher and then a ballroom-dancing teacher for much of her life. Now her husband was dead. She was broke and alone. She needed money.

The first thing Annie did was find someone to build her a barrel. She designed it herself. She added holes for air and straps on the inside so she could hold on.

The finished barrel was four and a half feet high. Annie named it the *Queen of the Mist*. It had a heavy iron weight attached to the bottom. The weight was supposed to keep the barrel stable in the water so it wouldn't flip over.

Then Annie hired someone to advertise her stunt so that crowds would come. She chose Frank Russell, a carnival man.

In October 1901, Frank arrived in Niagara Falls. Frank put Annie's barrel on display in a hotel lobby, to get people excited about her stunt.

Then he told the newspapers all about Annie—although he lied about her age. Annie made Frank promise to say she was only forty-two years old.

A few weeks later, on October 24, Annie arrived at the small island in the river. It was about a mile and a half above the edge of the falls. Photographers were standing by. They took pictures of the old woman in her long, dark dress and hat. Then they turned their backs so she could remove some of her clothes. Wearing only a short skirt and blouse, black stockings, and some slippers, she climbed into the barrel on her hands and knees.

Inside was a harness. It was sort of like a seat belt, to keep Annie from bouncing around. She strapped herself in and added some pillows to protect her from the bumps.

"So long, boys," Annie said.

The barrel lid was screwed on tight. A bicycle pump pumped air in through three holes. After that, the holes were sealed with corks, and a boatman rowed the barrel out into the Niagara River. But as he reached the right spot, the boatman heard Annie tapping on the barrel from inside.

"What is it?" he asked.

"The barrel is leaking," Annie said.

The boatman told her not to worry, and then he set the barrel—with Annie in it—loose.

"Good-bye," Annie said softly, as the *Queen of the Mist* headed toward the falls.

Would Annie survive?

CHAPTER 6
Defying Death

For about half an hour, Annie's barrel drifted peacefully downstream. But finally it reached the wild, rushing rapids that would toss her over the edge of Horseshoe Falls.

Horseshoe Falls was the biggest, most powerful waterfall at Niagara. Annie later said that the force of the water felt "like a thing of life, fighting for its prey."

By the time the barrel reached the brink of the waterfall, Annie was already banged up and bruised. Then there was a sudden moment of stillness. That meant she was right on the edge, almost going over. She had to hold on for dear life!

"Oh, Lord," Annie said.

The feeling of falling was terrible. Annie later said it felt like everything in nature was being destroyed.

Then all at once, everything was silent. Annie knew her barrel was underwater. Under the raging falls.

Would it ever come back up? Would it leak more? Would she have enough air to breathe?

For a full minute, she was held underwater.

Suddenly, the force of the rapids made the barrel shoot up ten or more feet into the air!

It landed with a crash, with Annie still inside. Then the rapids sent the barrel into the cavern behind the waterfall curtain. Annie was tossed about. For the next few moments, she was bashed by waves. The barrel was tossed into the air and dropped on the rocks. She wasn't sure if she would ever escape the whirlpool.

But finally, the barrel drifted downstream. Some men, including Carlisle Graham, were waiting on the nearby rocks. One of the men grabbed the rope attached to the barrel and pulled Annie to shore. She had been inside for almost an hour!

Was she alive?

When they opened the barrel, she waved at them feebly.

"Where am I?" she asked.

"You're over the falls," they told her.

Cold, dazed, and shaken, Annie did not have the strength to climb out of the barrel. They finally had to get a saw and cut part of the barrel away.

But Annie Taylor had survived the falls!
Thousands of people on both shores cheered
when they saw her dragged out of the barrel, alive.

The men helped her to her feet, wrapped her
in blankets, and took her to the room where she
was staying. A doctor came, but Annie was really
all right. She had a bad cut on her head, but no
broken bones. She just needed a few days' rest.

Annie had hoped to make some money from her famous trip. But although the newspapers wrote about her, no one seemed to want to meet her. People were disappointed that the daredevil was a gray-haired little old lady. They were more interested in seeing the barrel than in seeing her!

Frank Russell tried to help. He set up public appearances. Annie had to sit in store windows with her barrel. But no one made much money. Finally Frank stole her barrel from her and ran off!

Annie got her barrel back, and hired a new manager named William A. Banks. But he stole her barrel and ran off with it, too! Then he hired a pretty, young woman to pretend to be Annie. He knew he'd make more money that way!

For the rest of her life, Annie was poor. She had a copy of her barrel made. She traveled all over the world with it. But sometimes people didn't believe that she was really the person who had gone over the falls. She seemed too old.

When anyone asked about her trip over Niagara Falls, Annie had one piece of advice for them: "Don't try it." She said she would rather stand in front of a cannon and be blown to pieces than go over the falls again.

When she died in 1921, Annie was buried
in Oakwood Cemetery, near two other famous
Niagara Falls characters—the "barrel rider"
Carlisle Graham, and Francis Abbott, the Hermit
of Niagara Falls.

Nik Wallenda—Modern-Day Daredevil

These days, it's against the law to try to go over Niagara Falls in a barrel—or anything else! No one is allowed to walk a tightrope across the falls, either.

But Nik Wallenda was given special permission to do it in 2012. Nik was part of a famous circus family called the Flying Wallendas. The Flying Wallendas were known for tightrope-walking from very high places.

On a Friday night in June 2012, Nik began to walk across a two-inch-wide steel cable. He was heading to the Canadian side of the falls. His tightrope was 1,800 feet long—the length of six football fields! It was 200 feet above the falls.

Millions of people watched it live on TV. Winds were blowing hard. Would he fall? The TV network did not want to show a man falling to his death, so they made him wear a safety wire.

But Nik didn't slip. He even pranced for the last few steps. When he got to Canada, he had to show his passport to enter the country.

CHAPTER 7
Turning Water into Electricity

The force of Niagara Falls is more powerful than you can imagine. As much as 750,000 gallons of water drop over the edge of the falls every second! That much water weighs more than six million pounds! That's the same as if five hundred grand pianos, one thousand refrigerators, and nine hundred trucks all landed at once—and then the same number kept coming every second after that!

All that water has a lot of power in it. In fact, when Augustus Porter built the first water mill at Niagara Falls, he knew he could use only a tiny little bit of the waterfall. He built a small canal to direct some of the Niagara River off to the side. From there, the water in the canal turned a

waterwheel. If Porter had tried to put a waterwheel under Niagara Falls itself, the weight of the water would have smashed the wheel to pieces.

How a Waterwheel Works

Water falls from a cliff or runs downhill in a stream and hits a wheel with paddles. The force of the moving water makes the wheel turn. The wheel is connected to other moving parts through gears, ropes, and pulleys. So as the waterwheel turns, it makes the machinery move and do its work.

In a flour mill, for instance, the waterwheel can make a big stone go around. The stone grinds the wheat into flour. In a sawmill, the waterwheel makes a circular saw go around. The saw cuts logs into wooden boards.

Many people looked at Niagara Falls and wanted to use more of its power. Businessmen thought it was a huge waste to have all that water falling without putting it to work.

The question was: How could they turn Niagara's water into power?

The first to succeed was Jacob Schoellkopf. In 1877, he bought Augustus Porter's canal.

Jacob Schoellkopf

Then he ran several waterwheels at once, using the power of the falls. Each one sent power to a different business. A few years later, he used the water to run a small generator that lit up sixteen streetlights in Niagara Falls, New York.

Very few people had electric lights in those days. Thomas Edison had invented the first practical lightbulb in 1879. But at that time, there was no good way to get electricity into people's homes.

Why not? The
electricity that
Edison used
was called "direct
current." *Current* is
the word that refers to
electricity running through
wires. In those days, direct current

Thomas Edison

could travel only a short distance—a few miles.
For electric lights, there would have to be a better
way to get electricity to homes. Electricity would
have to travel for hundreds of miles—especially
if the power of Niagara Falls was going to be put
to work.

The Niagara Falls Power Company asked
Thomas Edison to help them solve the problem.
At first, Edison tried to help. But Edison was
stubborn. He refused to think about anything
other than direct current. His plans were too
expensive.

Meanwhile, a young man in Europe had come up with a different idea. His name was Nikola Tesla.

Nikola Tesla

Tesla was a genius. When he was four, he invented a waterwheel that would spin smoothly in water—without any paddles! He was so smart, he could memorize a page of facts just by looking at it once. As a teenager, he came up with some ideas about a new kind of electricity called "alternating current." Alternating current is the kind of electricity we use today. It can travel many miles from the place where it's created.

When he was twenty-eight years old, Nikola Tesla sailed to America and went to work for Thomas Edison. Tesla tried to convince Edison to use alternating current. But Edison wouldn't listen. He told Tesla, "Spare me that nonsense. It's dangerous. We're set up for direct current in America. People like it, and it's all I'll ever fool with."

Then Edison cheated Tesla out of some money he had promised to pay him!

So Tesla quit his job. He went to see another inventor named George Westinghouse. Westinghouse was a rival of Edison's. He liked the idea of alternating current. He paid Tesla a lot of money for his ideas. And he promised to pay Tesla $2.50 for every horsepower created. *Horsepower* is a term that defines the way electricity is measured. With this deal, Tesla was going to be rich!

George Westinghouse

Now the Niagara Falls Power Company knew they had a good way to send electricity to cities many miles away. So they dug a huge tunnel, more than a mile long, under the town of Niagara Falls. The tunnel gave them a way to change the path of some of the water. By shifting the water away from the falls, they could control the amount of water going over the falls, and use the rest for power. Tesla said it would create enough power to light every lamp in America!

It took a few years to finish building the power plant. When it was done in 1896, Tesla and Westinghouse came to Niagara Falls for a big ceremony. It was time to flip a switch and see if it worked. Would the electricity travel all the way to Buffalo, New York? Would Niagara Falls become famous for helping to light up the world?

The mayor of Buffalo wasn't sure, so he waited until midnight to flip the switch. If it didn't work, he didn't want people to know!

But the lights came on, and Tesla was a hero. Niagara Falls was famous! It was the first time electricity had been sent a long distance. Now people all over America could have electricity in their homes.

Tesla was rich, but he was generous, too. A year later, George Westinghouse came to ask Tesla a favor. The Westinghouse Company was going broke because they owed Tesla so much money. They had created so much horsepower, they owed him $12 million! Tesla agreed to give up his $2.50 payment for each horsepower in order to keep the Westinghouse Company from going bankrupt.

Today, the Westinghouse Company has become General Electric, or GE. And today, there is an electric car named for Nikola Tesla.

There is also a newer, modern power plant at Niagara Falls now. But it works pretty much the same way the old one did. Water from the Niagara River is diverted—forced to go off to the side—at the push of a button. It is sent through long, underground tunnels to the power plant. This means that people running the power plant can turn the water "down" on Niagara Falls. Or they can turn it up!

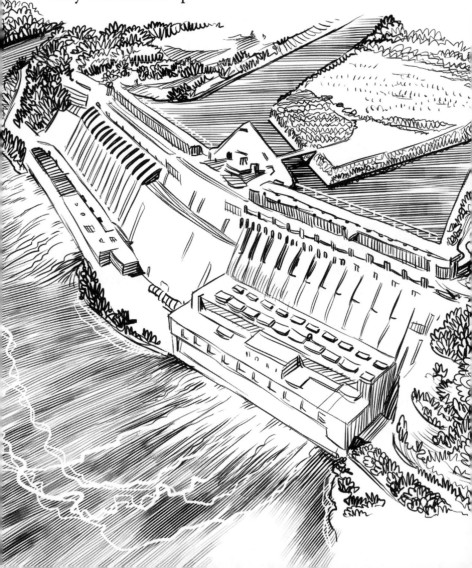

The United States and Canada have agreed
that they'll never turn the falls down too much,
though. They signed a treaty—an agreement.
It says that at least half the water from the river
should be allowed to flow over the falls during the
day, in tourist season. That way, people can enjoy
the beautiful sight. At night, when people are
sleeping, more of the water is used for electricity.

Since the water is always being turned down
some, no one today sees Niagara Falls the way it
used to look, hundreds of years ago. It's only half
as amazing as it used to be.

Erosion—Niagara Falls on the Move

Believe it or not, Niagara Falls is constantly moving south, little by little. Over the past five hundred years, the falls moved about three feet every year—or almost half a mile altogether! The falls may have moved as much as six feet in some years. In the course of fifteen thousand years, the actual location of Horseshoe Falls will be four miles from where it is now. In fifty thousand years, the falls will probably be gone!

Why?

The falls move because as the water flows over the edge of the gorge, it eats away at the rocky cliff. This is called erosion. You won't notice the change in a day or a week, but over time, the water is actually washing away the rock.

Imagine that you had a giant block of ice the size of a microwave oven. Now imagine that you poured hot water over one edge of the ice block. (Do not do this—just imagine it!) The heat would melt away the ice wherever it touched. Pretty soon, there would be a curved spot in the block of ice—just like Horseshoe Falls. If you kept pouring the hot water over that same place, the "edge" would keep melting away, and moving back. Eventually, the whole block of ice would be gone. That's what is happening to the rocky cliffs under the waterfalls at Niagara.

CHAPTER 8
Come to Niagara Falls

For more than 150 years, people have been visiting Niagara Falls. Often people came for their honeymoons. The more people came, the more the town of Niagara Falls tried to think up fun reasons for people to visit.

In 1899, the city built a huge castle made entirely out of ice! The ice palace had a tower that was fifty-five feet high. Inside was a huge skating rink. It was decorated with colored ice, and cakes made out of ice, with flowers frozen inside! Admission to the ice palace was sixty cents. The building lasted until February when the weather suddenly turned warm and it started to melt.

Some years, the waterfalls themselves have frozen solid! That used to happen a lot until the 1950s. Sometimes huge chunks of ice on the river would clump together, creating an "ice dam" or an "ice bridge." Then people could walk right across the frozen falls from America to Canada. Even in winter, tourists come from all over the world to see the falls.

Once, in 1883, a man built a shack out in the middle of the frozen ice bridge. He was right on the border between the United States and Canada—so he claimed he wasn't in either country. He said that meant he didn't have to follow any laws. He sold liquor from his shack, without a liquor license allowing him to do it!

In 1938, the ice froze on the river again. This time, the ice jammed against the two supports of a bridge called the Honeymoon Bridge. The bridge collapsed from the weight of the ice pushing against it. No one was hurt, though, because the bridge had been closed. Everyone knew it was going to fall down.

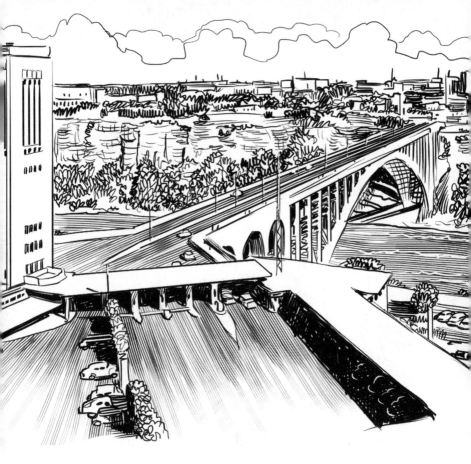

A new bridge, called the Rainbow Bridge, was built a few years later. It has a bell tower in it with a carillon. A carillon is a giant musical instrument with fifty-five huge bells. A person plays the bells by pressing keys and foot pedals, like the keys of a piano or an organ.

When it was built, the bell tower had a small apartment for someone to live in, so they could play the bells several times each day. Now the carillon is automated.

In 1953, a Hollywood movie was made about Niagara Falls. It starred a famous actress named Marilyn Monroe. In the story, a woman planned to murder her husband and have him thrown over Niagara Falls! The bell tower was used in the movie, too, as part of the murder plot.

Today, there is a lot to see in Niagara Falls. The
Maid of the Mist is one of the most popular rides. A
high-speed elevator takes people down the side of
the cliff, to the water. There, each person is given
a rain poncho with a hood. The boat takes people
so close to the falls, they usually get soaking wet.

Fun Facts about the Falls

- In the 1950s and '60s, teenagers had autograph books that their friends would sign. Girls often wrote "Yours till Niagara Falls" before they signed their names.

- The cereal called Shredded Wheat was first made and sold from Niagara Falls. There was a picture of the falls on the cereal box.

- The mist from Niagara Falls creates rainbows that can be seen even when it isn't raining!

- In 1969, the United States decided to stop the American Falls for a few months! Engineers built a dam to keep any water from flowing over the American side. They wanted to see what was underneath the falls, to make sure it was safe for boats. They also hoped to remove some rocks, so the waterfall would look more beautiful. Then they turned the falls back on.

- In 1931, a huge chunk of rock fell off the edge of the American Falls. It was so loud, it sounded like thunder thirty miles away!

- Fish travel over Niagara Falls—but even some of them can't survive the fall! About one out of every ten fish dies.

The Cave of the Winds is gone. It was closed up when rocks fell from the cliff and blocked the entrance. But people can walk up a long set of wooden walkways and stand very close to Bridal Veil Falls. You need more than a poncho for this trip, though. You need to wear a special pair of rubber shoes.

Goat Island is open to the public, too. And so
is the Rainbow Bridge. Fireworks are shot into
the air near the falls every week in the summer.

Both the American falls and the Canadian falls have all kinds of activities for families—a huge Ferris wheel, nature hikes, 3-D movies, a butterfly building, a giant clock made out of flowers, a lookout tower, aquariums, gardens, and more.

But the best reason to go to Niagara is the falls themselves. It may not be the tallest waterfall in the world. But nowhere else on earth can you see a waterfall with as much water rushing over it. It's one of America's most beautiful nature sites. And besides—if you don't hurry, Niagara Falls will be gone in about fifty thousand years!

What's the Biggest Waterfall in the World?

It's hard to say which waterfall is the biggest. It depends on how you measure. Some are tall but have only a trickle of water. Some are wide and have a ton of water flowing over them. Some are so deep in the jungle, it's hard to even measure them at all! Here's a list of five of the most amazing waterfalls in the world.

1. Victoria Falls in Africa on the border of Zambia and Zimbabwe

Not the tallest or the widest, but this waterfall is considered the biggest in the world, because it has the biggest curtain of falling water. At 354 feet tall, it's twice as tall as Niagara. It's also more than a mile wide!

2. Niagara Falls in the US and Canada

More water flows over Niagara than any other tall waterfall—twice as much as Victoria Falls!

Victoria Falls in Africa

Yosemite Falls in California

3. Iguazu Falls on the border of Brazil and Argentina

This waterfall is actually a bunch of smaller falls—275 in all! Together, they are almost two miles wide.

4. Angel Falls in Venezuela

One of the tallest in the world at 3,212 feet, this waterfall lies deep in the rainforest.

5. Yosemite Falls in California

One of the tallest waterfalls in the world, it's 2,425 feet tall—almost half a mile high!

Timeline of Niagara Falls

c. 8000 BC	Niagara Falls is formed
1678	Father Hennepin is the first white man to see the falls
1751	Swedish visitor Pehr Kalm's diary is printed in English; it contains a description of Niagara Falls
1814	Augustus Porter buys land near Niagara Falls
1829	Francis Abbott, "the Hermit of Niagara," arrives
	Sam Patch, "the Jersey Jumper," leaps into the falls
1848	Homan Walsh flies a kite across the Niagara River to help build the first bridge
	Niagara Falls suddenly goes dry
1855	Suspension bridge designed by John Roebling opens over the Niagara River
1859	Blondin walks across the gorge on a tightrope
1860	Farini performs stunts on a tightrope across the gorge
1877	Jacob Schoellkopf uses the falls to run several waterwheels that create electricity
1896	Niagara Falls Power Company sends electricity to Buffalo
1899	Ice palace is built as part of winter festival in Niagara
1901	Annie Edson Taylor goes over Niagara Falls in a barrel
1941	Rainbow Bridge is built to replace the Honeymoon Bridge that collapsed
1960	Seven-year-old Roger Woodward survives going over Niagara Falls
2012	Nik Wallenda walks across the gorge on a tightrope on live television

Timeline of the World

Last Ice Age ends	c. 9600 BC
First horse race in North America takes place in New York	1668
The Lewis and Clark Expedition begins in St. Louis, Missouri	1804
The Lewis and Clark Expedition reaches the Pacific Ocean	1805
The United States declares war on Great Britain and Ireland; the War of 1812 begins	1812
First steam locomotive is introduced	1825
Texas declares independence from Mexico	1836
Frederick Douglass publishes *Narrative of the Life of an American Slave*	1845
American Civil War begins	1861
American Civil War ends	1865
First Kentucky Derby takes place	1875
New Zealand becomes the first country to give women the right to vote	1893
World War I begins in Europe	1914
World War I ends	1918
German airship *Hindenburg* explodes while landing in New Jersey	1937
Thurgood Marshall becomes the first African American on the US Supreme Court	1967
NASA spacecraft lands on Mars	1997
Malala Yousafzai becomes the youngest winner of the Nobel Peace Prize, at seventeen	2014

Bibliography

*Books for young readers

Berton, Pierre. *Niagara: A History of the Falls*. Toronto: McClelland & Stewart, 1992.

Gromosiak, Paul and Christopher Stoianoff. *Images of America: Niagara Falls 1850–2000*. Charleston, SC: Arcadia, 2012.

* Van Allsburg, Chris. *Queen of the Falls*. Boston: Houghton Mifflin Harcourt, 2011.

CANADA

QUEEN ST

MORRISON ST

VICTORIA AVE.

NIAGARA
FALLS

RAINBOW
BRIDGE

NIAGARA ST

AMERICAN
FALLS

BRIDAL
VEIL
FALLS

GREEN
ISLAND

SKYLON
TOWER

CAVE OF
THE WINDS

GOAT
ISLAND

HORSESHOE
FALLS

THREE SISTERS
ISLANDS

DUFFERIN
ISLANDS

Aerial view of the falls

Niagara Falls and fireworks

Maid of the Mist

Visitors at Niagara Falls